In His Grip

My Story of God's Rescue and Redemption

NANCY CROWTHER-BRANDENBURG

Foreword by Todd Stryd, MDiv. PsyD

Edited by Justin Michael Brandenburg

WestBow Press books may be ordered through booksellers or by contacting:

WestBow Press
A Division of Thomas Nelson & Zondervan
1663 Liberty Drive
Bloomington, IN 47403
www.westbowpress.com
844-714-3454

Because of the dynamic nature of the Internet, any web addresses or links contained in this book may have changed since publication and may no longer be valid. The views expressed in this work are solely those of the author and do not necessarily reflect the views of the publisher, and the publisher hereby disclaims any responsibility for them.

Any people depicted in stock imagery provided by Getty Images are models, and such images are being used for illustrative purposes only.
Certain stock imagery © Getty Images.

Scripture quotations marked (ESV) are from the ESV® Bible (The Holy Bible, English Standard Version®), copyright © 2001 by Crossway, a publishing ministry of Good News Publishers. Used by permission. All rights reserved.

ISBN: 978-1-6642-9176-8 (sc)
ISBN: 978-1-6642-9177-5 (e)

Library of Congress Control Number: 2023902298

Print information available on the last page.

WestBow Press rev. date: 02/15/2023

WESTBOW
PRESS®
A DIVISION OF THOMAS NELSON
& ZONDERVAN

CONTENTS

ACKNOWLEDGEMENTS

As you will see from my past five years of work through my poems, God provided a person to walk with me through my story of many hard years and that work continues. Scripture was shared with me in a way I had never understood before and the person of Jesus Christ was revealed to me. I've realized that I do have a personal relationship with our loving Savior.

I offer many thanks to the churches where I and my family worshiped during these past few years: Cornerstone OPC of Ambler, PA, Glenside New Life, Calvary OPC, Glenside, PA and Bridge Community Church of Glenside, PA. I want to thank their pastors, elders, deacons, and friends all who prayed for and supported me and my sons and daughter through these last five years.

My love goes out to my sons and daughter, Justin, Jonathan, Jeremy, Jared and Kirsten and my daughter-in laws, Jenifer, Alex and Kourtney as well as my son-in-law Carl, for prayers, working together for my rescue in 2016, supporting me, even providing a place for me to live throughout 2016 and 2017. A special thanks to my youngest son, Jared who I have lived with the past three years, and he has persevered with me through some hard, emotion filled days. Another special thanks goes to my oldest son, Justin, who agreed to read and edit my work here, which I am sure was difficult for him at times.

Special love and appreciation to my sons and daughter for the sadness I feel about how our life together looked. Many times, I am sure you have asked God why our lives had to look like this but know that as hard as this was, God was with us, holding our hand and delivering us from an unjust, cruel man as He promised. Although his imprint will remain to some degree through our lives, the work we do will help soften it.

My love and appreciation goes out to family and friends who God brought back to us after many years of being cut off, as well as some new friends God brought to us in recent years. Many thanks for your prayers and support through these last five years. In counseling I learned to trust this safe inner circle, many of whom remain close. My brother, Bill and his wife Lori, stepsisters: Chiyo, Diohn, Fawn, my cousin Sue; close friends: Susan, Steve, Janet, Deb, Erin and John. A very special thanks and remembrance goes to my stepmother, Mef for her love and prayers over these last years after we reconnected. Jesus called her home July 17, 2022. Her gentle, loving spirit is sorely missed.

Extending loving thoughts to any women and their children who have suffered abuse at the hands of the person called to love them. I will pray for women in the healing process and courage for others to bring their story to light.

O Israel, hope in the Lord! For with
the Lord there is steadfast love, and
with him is plentiful redemption
Psalm 130:7

FOREWORD

In this compilation of poems and prose Nancy Brandenburg chronicles her journey through the horrors of abuse as she desperately clings to the right hand of her Father in Heaven. Her writing leads the reader through her process of breaking free from lies, working to build a new life, and ultimately finding the permission and opportunity to flourish as God's child. She eloquently captures the simple yet profound truth that Jesus walks with his people through the incomprehensible and insurmountable. Nancy's story reminds us that because God does not forsake his people, He never ceases to be at work behind the darkness. Escape is possible. Redemption is possible. Flourishing is possible.

Todd Stryd, MDiv. PsyD

PREFACE

This is the story of a woman and her children. It is a story of love and redemption from abuse and humiliation. There is fear, sadness and grief written here but you will see God's protection and love as he redeems hearts and minds for His own glory. I am this woman and the children, my four sons and daughter. You will see how God prepared me for my work for His kingdom through hard things in my childhood. He walked along side me, holding my right hand, preserving my children and I body and soul.

My story is written in a mixture of poetry and prose. Through biblical counseling and processing my past, poetry became my outlet to speak about hard things. So, each poem has its own story in God's promise of redemption.

My goal in writing this is to demonstrate how an abuser's power and control damages the hearts and minds of those he is called to love. Also, often this happens in secret, for many years before being brought to light. You will see how God opened scripture to me as He worked for my rescue. As I started to see my life through the lens of scripture, I began processing years of abuse through much painful, hard work. God gave me a person and place to counsel me in my walk to freedom, and for that I am very thankful.

My prayer for you, as you read, is to help you see that this could be any woman, your neighbor, sister, church member, coworker, anyone you pass in the street because it is done in secret. I do not mean for the reader to be suspicious of everyone but to be ready to offer help and reach out. A woman may only need one safe person to confide in to bring her abuse to light. I will pray for the courage of many to see and help so, one woman at a time can be rescued from their oppressor.

If you are a pastor or elder, reading this and a woman comes to you, please believe her. Know that the shame she feels to seek help is now less than the fear of staying in her abusive situation. In a sermon in April 2016, Dr. Carl Trueman said, "In a church of 100 people there is at least one wife being abused by their husband."[1] Some people will ask "why did you stay" or "you supported him." These are common misunderstandings of oppression and abuse. I wanted to believe the man's public persona because the reality of what happened in the privacy of our home was too hard to accept, to shameful to admit. I will refer to him as "the man" because he was neither a husband nor father as God intended.

For purposes of my story, I will be referring to women because the majority of abuse is men towards women. Lundy Bancroft, in his book "Why Does He Do That" states, "Two to four million women are assaulted by their partner every year in the U.S. That is excluding verbal and mental abuse. Domestic abuse is the number one cause of injury to women."[2] Abuse is about power, he says and is demonstrated verbally, psychologically, physically, and sexually, even financially. An alarming part of these statistics is that only about 30% of those with injuries seek medical help. Women do not want to bring abuse to light. They want to stay hidden. I have spoken to several women who, like me never went to the police. Women who did reach out to their churches, as I did in 1991 but did not receive the help they desperately needed. Women who cannot speak of their abuse, trying to leave it in the past. God has given me the strength to tell my story to make it real for people who doubt or a woman still living in her oppression. My work here also, helps me put my painful memories to rest and softens my emotional scars.

If this story is yours, I will pray for you to seek help. In his sermon, "Beauty and the Beast" July 10, 2016, Dr.Liam Goligher, Senior Pastor of Tenth Presbyterian Church, Philadelphia said, "God does not want a woman to remain in an abusive relationship so that he can use her there."[3] God seeks out the lowly in heart and provides rest for your soul.

> *"Wait for the Lord; be strong and let your heart take courage; wait for the Lord"*!
> *Psalm 27:14, ESV*

This was a verse that helped me when I was able to leave the man. Take heart, God will direct your path.

Some of my favorite quotes come from Corrie Ten Boom. She was a woman who suffered greatly and knew Jesus love for her and his presence in her suffering. This quote has been an encouragement in my healing because I saw how God prepared me for my path in life.

> *"This is what the past is for! Every experience God gives us,*
> *every person he puts in our lives is the perfect preparation*
> *for the future that only he can see."*[4]

As a young child I experienced a loss and sadness and God used that to give me strength in my weakness for my path in life.

> *"The steps of a man are established by the Lord,*
> *when he delights in his way"*
> *Psalm 37:23, ESV*

Thank you for taking time to read my story. I pray it will be a blessing, as you see God's work of redemption in my family's lives.

Nancy Crowther-Brandenburg
January 21, 2022

REDEEMED

My life began in the middle of the Baby Boom in 1954. Post WWII events were in full swing: the Supreme Court ruled that race based segregation in schools is unconstitutional, Joseph McCarthy conducted televised inquiries into communist infiltration of the Army, increasing global concern of nuclear fallout, Jonas Salk began immunizing children with the polio vaccine, Billy Graham was seeing an increased interest in Christian revival, and Category 4 Hurricane Hazel made landfall in North Carolina and it's destruction is carried through the mid-Atlantic States up into New York with 100 mile per hour winds. It sounds very similar to what life is like now in the early 2020's. There is conflict in international, national, and local news. There is work being done with vaccines, hurricanes bringing destruction, equal justice and racial concerns, and people are looking to Christ for answers and faith. God is in the details of our lives.

I was born into the family of William and Elizabeth Crowther, along with my older brother Billy. Living in a home nestled among the farmland of Bucks County, Pennsylvania, life seemed idyllic. Loving parents, in a home with many memories of aunts, uncles and cousins visiting. We spent our days at family dinners, caring for the family dog, running through corn fields, and climbing our backyard Weeping Willow tree. Until, on that beautiful, sunny, summer day when tragedy struck so unexpectedly, and everything changed.

For he will hide me in his shelter in the
day of trouble; he will conceal me under the cover
of his tent, he will lift me high upon a rock.
Psalm 27:5, ESV

Weeping may tarry for the night but,
joy comes with the morning.
Psalm 30:5, ESV
A little girl
Lost her mother

But Jesus was there
He held her hand
Dried her tears
Wrote His word on her heart
He knew this little girl
God would ask hard things of her
But…
He would be her fortress…. her refuge
He would love her…. comfort her
His hands pierced for her
The little girl had dreams
She would care for people… love them
Looked forward to marriage… children
It would be hard
God called her to this work
He was there in her weakness
She prayed and trusted him
There would be plentiful redemption
God gave her courage for the work
Courage for the waiting
Though pieces are still cracked
She will pray and wait for it all…
To be redeemed
I was that little girl

IN HIS GRIP

Tragedy did strike on that summer day when I was six. I watched my mom crying, holding her chest in pain. That was the last time I saw her. The doctors came and I remember sitting with them but not what they said. I asked, "can't you bring her back?" Dad was carrying me and holding my brother's hand. Even as a little girl I saw the sadness in my dad's face. He had lost a part of himself. He made the hard decision to sell our home and move to Roxborough, in the northwest section of Philadelphia, to live with our paternal grandmother. There we would have support from both of our grandmothers, aunts and uncles and would also be close to our cousins. His wife, our mother was taken so soon, and life had drastically changed.

Roxborough was a timeless neighborhood in the sixties. Friends running and playing in the streets: wall ball, jacks, hide and seek. Back in a time when neighbors helped each other. Our home was filled with love. Sunday School and family gatherings on holidays continued. My sadness came in the early morning hours, praying God would not take Dad too. Dad did all the mom things: Girl Scouts, cookie sales, sleepovers as he tried to insure I didn't miss anything. He encouraged me to follow my dream to become a nurse, which I did. He was also there by my side to walk me down the aisle, as I fulfilled my heart's desire to be married and have a family full of love like my parents had. My wedding was a beautiful celebration of my love for the man. However, I would soon realize that I was "in his grip."

So many years ago
It seems like a different lifetime
My heart's desire
Was to be married
To be loved by my husband
As God intended
I saw my parents
Loving each other
Tender, sweet communion
Our home filled with joy and love
Sadness came quickly, unexpectedly
Dad was heartbroken
Lost his soulmate
Part of himself was gone
This heaven-sent love
Was my heart's desire
So… I waited
He seemed a man of faith
Loving
Caring
Tender
My journey in marriage began
His anger, abandonment came quickly
I was in his grip
Anger turned to rage
He breathed out violence
Unfaithful
Coercive…
I lost myself
God rescued me from the grasp of…
A wicked
Unjust
Cruel man
My story of rescue and redemption begins…

NEW LIFE

My abuse started on our honeymoon. I did not see it as abuse for many years. I had taken vows, made a commitment before God. Yelling on the honeymoon escalated to physical abuse by the end of our first year of marriage after my first son was born. I had been told he had a "bad temper", and I was encouraged to think of *Proverbs 15:1 "A soft answer turns away wrath, but a harsh word stirs up anger."* Now I see that God used that verse to protect me and my children many times over because I was able to remain silent and not inflame violent situations.

By my third year of marriage, I realize now, I was alone, but I did not know what to do or how to do it. Shame kept me from speaking up, seeking help. There was all manner of abuse at this point, including unfaithfulness. Many nights I would cry, alone in my bed, thinking I had married Dr. Jekyll and Mr. Hyde. Lundy Bancroft's book, "Why Does He Do That" was recommended to me and I found comfort when the first sentence in his book is a quote he heard from many women, "He's two different people. I feel like I am living with Dr. Jekyll and Mr. Hyde."[5] On my hardest days, I even thought of taking the man's Valium. I would repent for that many times because I had two sons now. As I have said it is helpful for me to refer to him as "the man" because he was neither a husband nor father, as God intended.

Many years went by, and this is my first poem. I wrote this right before I got out in 2016. God gave me two verses that I meditated on to leave my husband. Through God's word *"out of the abundance of the heart the mouth speaks "* Luke 6:45, this was the man's heart that spoke and *"For nothing is hidden that will not be made manifest, nor is anything secret that will not be known and come to light"* Luke 8:17, I needed to bring my story to light. God rescued me.

Early in 2020, my youngest son and I were having a conversation about my rescue. I said, "God really did rescue me because I was in a desperate place emotionally and I had no ability to get out." Jared said, "Mom we were all rescued because we couldn't continue to watch you dying inside." My four sons and daughter and their spouses had prayed for a way to get me out since 2011. God moved quickly in 2016. I wrote this poem the week I left.

On that summer day so long ago
The Lord took my mother home
So young was I… I never asked
Why Lord
Why me
Why now
The Lord was gentle, always kind
He saved me from my sin
Provided, loved, and walked with me
Through this life
That he has given
He sent his Spirit, Comforter
To… exhort, rebuke, sustain
And now I pray His gentle hand
Will bring me peace within

MY SEASON OF WAITING

In my eleventh year of marriage, 1991, I left for the first time. On Mother's Day at a family brunch an abusive incident was witnessed by others. A person close to me called the next day to check on me and I shared stories of abuses from the past several years. She said, "you and the children need to leave." This thought had never occurred to me. She came that day while the man was at work, helped me pack up, I called my church, and the pastoral staff became involved, and we left. My pastor arranged for me to meet a counselor, the pastor talked to the man, we all met together at the end of the week and the pastor said, "we could go home, it is safe." I was on my own again, living the lie that all was well, and I needed to make this work. There was no follow up from my church. The man never saw a counselor. Two months later at the end of a busy day the man was in such a rage that he headbutted me and I had two black eyes in the morning. The next day we left on a two week vacation and I wore sunglasses all day, every day. At the end of the first week the man was angry with me that my eyes weren't healing quickly enough. I was on my own and "my season of waiting" had begun.

You may be thinking, how did my church send me home? How did they not follow up? The Church was very weak on abuse, it was 1991 and would only allow for separation and divorce with unfaithfulness. In recent years there has been much education of Church leadership from men and women educated and trained as biblical counselors. The Church's response and care for women is changing. The safety of the woman and children need to be the primary concern not the stability of the marriage. Early in counseling, Psalm 31:21 and Isaiah 41:13 were shared with me.

Blessed be the Lord, for he has wondrously
shown his steadfast love
to me when I was in a besieged city.
Psalm 31:21, ESV

For I, the Lord your God, hold your right hand;
it is I who say to you, "fear not, I am
the one who helps you."
Isaiah 41:13, ESV

The imagery of these metaphors helped inspire this poem. This is one of my earliest poems and there would be much hard work processing my abuse going forward. I would ponder these verses many times and they will be seen in other poems. In our weakness God knows we need to be reminded many times of the promises of scripture: that His steadfast love is sure, he holds our hand and many other examples of his protection and care for us. My work had begun in processing "my season of waiting."

It was a season of love
A season of pain
It was a season of joy
A season of sorrow
It was my season of waiting
Through many tomorrows
The Lord was there, His steadfast love, assured
In His hiding place he held my hand
To comfort my tears and fears
It was my season of waiting
I wanted to flee
The Lord answered, no
He had work for me
He gave me the joy of His word
His sweet communion
He gave me joy in my children
His sweet consolations
It was my season of waiting
But His redemption was freeing
He opened a door, held my hand, I came to Him
My tomorrows are yesterday's
Moving forward with Jesus
This is my season of waiting
Living with Him through this life
Freedom He gave me to deliver me from strife
I trust the path He has laid for me
I will live it for Him, completely

SCRIPTURES LENSE

I was in a safe place with my biblical counselor who was gentle and honest with me. This would be painful, hard work and I had freedom to share my story at my pace and was encouraged to repeat things as needed to quiet the memories. Many times, at counseling, it was my counselor's silence and patience or just a few words that allowed me time to speak about hard things. My counselor opened scripture to me so that it came alive, and I saw God in the details of my life. There are several times through counseling that I envisioned life as my jail with no bars or key. My counselor explained the jail was in my mind. I could see that and at times it was so confining it almost felt palpable.

One day in early 2020, I came to counseling and said, "I am seeing my life through the lens of scripture." Shortly after that I wrote this poem on one of my walks. As my counseling progressed, it may have been a scripture verse or just one word that inspired my poems. Most of my poems were written on walks because it was a safe place for me.

God's word shining through a crystal lens
Light breaks through the darkness
My darkness
I see the lies exposed
God's truth, revealing
Oppression
Pain
Humiliation
Fear
It was my jail
All consuming
God's word my light
His truth my key
It was not my fault
I did not deserve it
We did not deserve it
But God was there
I see my life through the lens
Steadfast love when besieged
God present, in our fear
Cleansed our humiliation
Promises justice for oppression
Our new story emerging
Brought out into this broad, safe place
A new song of thanks in my heart
My story of God's rescue and redemption
Through scripture's lens

WHO AM I?

Seven months after I left in 2016, I joined the man in counseling with a person who had been working with him. This was not helpful for me, I was labeled an avoider with PTSD because my mother died when I was six. I had limited time to speak and was prohibited from speaking of my abuse. One day I just got up and walked out and asked my pastor to connect me with a biblical counselor. So, I started with my new biblical counselor in November 2017. The most important thing in the first session was I knew my counselor saw the truth of my story and asked, "When could I come back?" I knew this would be a safe place for me.

In counseling, as I started to process memories or flashbacks, they came so quickly, I referred to them as "my slideshow." The feeling of having no control over how fast they came or when they came was troubling. I saw how, during my marriage I was on high alert for episodes of anger turning to rage towards my children and myself. The man used tactics to make me feel like I was off balance emotionally and didn't understand what was happening. It was explained to me that abusers use brainwashing to control their spouse. I lost myself. Through this poem, I was able to pull those thoughts and feelings together.

Lundy Bancroft speaks of a process called "traumatic bonding". The "assaults that an abuser makes on the women's self-opinion, his undermining of her progress in life, the wedges he drives between her and other people, the psychological effects left on her when he turns scary - all combine to cause her to *need him more and more*. This is a bitter psychological irony."[6]

Born a daughter, a sister
God knew me
Called my name
Time passed
I became a woman
God still knew me
I knew myself
Found love …. I thought
I became a wife, a mother
God still knew me
But I lost myself
Who was I
I see myself, loving my children
But there is chaos
Life is unpredictable
I am cut off
What is true
I am confused
I cannot catch my breath
God still knew me
Kept me safe
Called me back to Him
His word is drawing me out
Freeing my mind, my heart
I can see myself…
A daughter, sister, and mother
God knows me
The woman he called me to be
Safe in His everlasting arms
Living for Him

NOT ALONE

All through the first few years of counseling I have seen that I was alone in my marriage. I see my effort to be loved, diffuse anger, try to hold our family together, all at a cost to my children and myself. Late in 2020 I was struggling and on an emotional roller coaster because the divorce was taking so long and new divisions had arisen amongst my four sons and daughter. My counselor shared Psalm 124 which I used for the next week in my devotions. Portions I will share with you to show how the metaphors were encouraging and calmed my thoughts.

> *If it had not been the Lord who was on our side…then (he)*
> *would have swallowed us up alive, then the flood would have*
> *gone over us…Blessed be the Lord, who has not given us*
> *as prey to (his) teeth! We have escaped like a bird…the*
> *snare is broken and we have escaped! Our help is in the*
> *name of the Lord…*
>
> Psalm 124, ESV

In our lives, especially in our suffering, it is okay to ask the why question. I was always afraid that would mean I didn't trust God; it would be sinful. I have learned that I can cry out to God in my distress and ask, *"Lord, how long?"* During my marriage I was alone many times. I needed a loving husband as God intended. There were three miscarriages, the death of my dad, injuries, a car accident on my way to work and the loving warmth and compassion that a godly husband would give could have truly helped during those traumatic moments. Instead, I was very alone in an "earthly" sense.

We had a wedding
It was a beautiful, joyful day
God promised unity of our hearts
I would be his loving helper
He would nourish and cherish me
And then I was alone…
But …I had spoken vows
Promises before God
I submitted to His will
And…surrendered to the man
I see now…
God was on my side
He did not let the rage overtake me
The Lord was my hiding place
With trouble all around me
The Lord was with me
I waited…God set me free
Escaped, like a bird from his grip
I am by myself now
But…not alone

INTRO TO POEMS FOR MY CHILDREN:

God blessed me with four sons and a daughter, Justin, Jonathan, Jeremy, Kirsten, and Jared - in that order. Justin is seven-and-a-half years older than Jared. I suffered three miscarriages and experienced much grief about those babies for many years. God gave me the joy of motherhood. I was both a mother and protector. Lundy Bancroft, in his book, "Why Does He Do That", states that, "a man who abuses his partner is seven times more likely to abuse the children."[7] That was the case for us.

When I left in 1991, I shared stories of my abuse and my children to our pastor and the counselor I met with once. I shared serious incidents of abuse. Despite that we were sent home with no follow up and the abuse continued. My thoughts were, "I need to make this work to keep us safe." After God rescued me in 2016, it gave my now adult children the freedom to share their own stories that I had no knowledge of. We suffered abuse together and individually. Bancroft also states that an abuser does this to keep everyone off balance to retain control. He goes to great lengths to pit the children against each other.

In 2016 I asked my sons and daughter if they were upset that we did not leave when they were younger. They all said, "it would have been worse for us to be alone with him." My youngest son, Jared, said that "my goal and everything I did was done to try to prevent him from getting angry." It would have been difficult to prevent the man from having partial custody. The laws are not written in the best interest of the children. Mothers need considerable evidence, or it is his word against her word. The children's testimony many times is not accepted by the court for various reasons. Even in 2022, the court remains weak in the protection of women and children, giving partial custody of the children to men who have abused their partners despite the women having Protection From Abuse orders from the court.

Jennifer Michelle Greenberg has spoken very powerfully against abuse to the OPC and PCA churches. One of her quotes resonates with me "If my story shines light in the darkness, I will repeat it until the darkness is afraid."[8] I also, think it is important for me to tell our story until I am not afraid of it. Healing makes us survivors, not victims. My fear was paralyzing for many years, but God was the strength in my weakness. These poems come from many thoughts and prayers for my, now, adult children and their healing.

SONS

Baby boys first, each different at birth
So sweet, but so brief you can snuggle and hold
They grow so quick and off they go
To imaginary battles, castles and play in the snow
You see in their faces the love of adventure
Digging and searching for some ancient treasure
As time marches on and they grow into men
You pray for God to know them for Him
They have seen and have suffered things that should not have been
God's shelter was over them
His shadow and shield
My sons, all four He brought out of that darkness
Though they still struggle at times
They will flourish through His loving kindness

THE KEY TO HER HEART

She is my daughter born brave and beautiful
Known first by our Heavenly father
Who holds the key
She was a gift to love and nurture
Because of what I could not see
He held the key that kept her heart
Brave and loving and joyful
Her smile so sweet, her eyes so knowing
The Lord sustained her with steadfast loving
She is now, a woman grown
Still brave and beautiful through Him alone
His word is the key, His love so sweet
She trusts in Him who holds the key
He will provide in any season
His love is sure and freely given

IMPRINT

In early 2020 I was struggling with traumatic memories returning of my abuse. The image of my jail with no escape had returned. There was a day in May 2020 when the tears would not stop from the memories and things currently happening in my personal life. My counselor had previously shared the word "imprint", explaining that the abuser leaves an imprint on those he abuses. I thought of a fossil and how the fish or animals imprint are left permanently on the rocks. The word "imprint" gave me a concrete metaphor to think about my abuse and how to put words to it within the construct of my healing.

Because scripture speaks to everything in our lives, I did a search of the word imprint. It is used in some translations more than others. The ESV and NIV exchange the word imprint for mark, write, and remember. Some months after my counseling session I wrote this poem on my walk and "imprint" seemed the best way for me express my thoughts and feelings at the time.

He left a dark imprint on my mind
It is deep and painful
The memories come hard and fast
If I could just make them stop
I see myself and he is there
But my mind is elsewhere
It is not good, I don't want to be there
I cannot say no
Those times are over
But his imprint remains
There are still hard days
Finding words to peel away the darkness
I hear Jesus say, "look"
Your imprint is on my palms
My Father made you; you are mine
My word imprinted on your heart
Know my steadfast love is everlasting
And….
My light overcomes the darkest imprint

SHAME

"With all humility and gentleness, with patience,
Bearing with one another in love, eager
To maintain the unity of the Spirit in the bond of peace"
Ephesians 4:2-3, ESV

This verse was how I approached my wedding day. This was my hope. And then it was not. Doing everything I could to receive love in return and not receive it produces shame and humiliation as a result of continuous belittling, yelling, physical abuse, unfaithfulness, and all manner of controlling my thoughts and world. Reliving this while processing it in counseling was painful, hard work.

The day my counselor shared Psalm 31:21 about being besieged, I went home and thought and prayed about that for several days. This is something someone who is kidnaped or a prisoner of war experiences, not the wife of a "believer". In another counseling session I was able to put words to this. I was cut off, isolated and could not think for myself. My mind was held captive. Metaphors of scripture, like Psalm 31:21 were helpful in my healing.

Because I am a nurse, I used medical images as metaphors to explain my shame and humiliation. Serious wounds sometimes get infected and need to be debrided. This is a procedure to clean and remove infected or necrotic skin. I imagined this painful process to help me envision the peeling away of the dark memories. Another image I thought of was the amputation of a diseased limb and having phantom pain that continues. I needed examples of concrete images to do the hard work of putting words to my memories.

Psalm 129 was also shared with me during counseling. I imagined the *"long furrows upon my back"*, deep and painful. If you continue in the Psalm, God *"cuts the cords of the wicked"* and then move on to Psalm 130 *"my soul waits for the Lord more than watchmen in the morning"* and *"with him there is plentiful redemption"*. Go to Psalm 131 and God *"calms and quiets my soul"*. I used these Psalms many nights when shame would not leave me.

You may notice that my poems are not in chronological order from the time when God rescued me but, rather, as I processed things in counseling. There are times in my poems that I repeat words used previously. As memories resurface, sometimes I needed to speak about them again. We are human and God repeats His promises for us many times. Poems gave me the words to quiet my thoughts and memories. I had been doing some hard work in counseling sessions in January 2020 and hence this poem was a product of that.

Shame is dark
Dirty
Cuts deep
I am alone
Exposed
Hiding inside
Everyone knows
Sees me
Crying inside
No one hears
Understands
I wanted the pain to stop
Wanted to make it stop
Death would have been better
God called my name
He heard my cry
Steadfast love is mine
I called on Jesus
He took my pain
Dried my tears
His blood was shed for me
I stand in his righteousness
Cleansed with His blood
And I am free

SADNESS AND HEALING

Although these two poems were written a few months apart they are connected for me in my heart and mind. Processing the things that happened is sometimes more difficult than living in the abuse. Late in 2020 I asked my counselor how I was able to remain completely calm when, for example, he had his fists on my jaw threatening to break it or knock all my teeth out. My counselor explained that I was able to dissociate from the immediate threat and remain calm to be able to function, care for my children, work as a nurse. In a later session I said that it seems God gave us protective ways for our brains to keep us safe.

Memories come in unpredictable waves and healing is a continuum. There are times they are more pronounced, and I needed to do the hard work of "putting words to my trauma." On September 13, 2019, I wrote in my journal that there are kinds of abuse that cut deep like a knife, reopen, and do not heal due to the shame. As I spoke about things, sometimes more than once, the wounds need debriding, again. The scars soften and the memories quiet. "Putting words to things", continues to be the painful hard work I needed to do to be free. These poems were inspired by two verses in the Psalms.

But you, O Lord, are a shield about me, my glory, and The lifter of my head.
Psalm 3:3, ESV

Keep me as the apple of your eye; and hide me in the shadow of our wings.
Psalm 17:8, ESV

SADNESS

Sad today
Comes in waves
Powerful, unpredictable
Holds me down
My mind still held captive
Memories persist
God lifted my head
Drew me out
The winter sun, bright
God's blue sky, cloudless
I see his steadfast love
His everlasting arms holding me
His promises, true
He leads my way
Gives me …
Rest
Strength
Hope
In my trials in life
His love lifted me
My joy returns

HEALING

My heart is heavy
The memories came quickly
Tears flowed freely
Walking on the crisp, sunny day
God was near
He heard me call
My heart was troubled
He walked with me
He knew my distress
I see clearly now…
He was… in our midst
Under the shadow of his wings
We hid in plain site
He rescued us
His ways and time perfect
The wounds are healing
The scars will soften
As I walked
He lifted my burdens
For his goodness
Because of his steadfast love

GOODNESS

Memories that made me feel not good enough, in despair or wanting to be invisible recycle through my mind on occasion. I like to use the word "recycle" because it is a good metaphor I can use to recover cleanliness or purity. I often wrestle with being good and pure and clean. When the verbal assaults or other memories, "recycle", I can use scripture to cleanse the evil.

When my thoughts turned to these feelings, my counselor shared these verses and God's word gradually became louder than the memories that I wanted me to believe I was not good enough. When my mind goes to these thoughts, even now in 2022, I use these verses to remind me of the truth.

"And to Jesus, the mediator of a new covenant
and to the sprinkled blood that speaks a
better word than the blood of Abel".
Hebrews 12:24, ESV

"For whenever our heart condemns us,
God is greater than our heart, and knows
everything."
1 John 3:20, ESV

I do not feel good
Need to stay hidden
Satan says "despair"
"You are not good"
"deserve to be punished"
This was my struggle, until…
God said, "no"
See Jesus on the cross
He took it all… for me
Do not hide my light
My Spirit is in you
People need to see
Scripture says, "let my light shine"
For His glory, His goodness
I will do the work
To cleanse the shame
To let God's light shine…
…In me

GOD'S PLEASURE

One of the difficult things to work on for me was turning off the humiliating, criticizing words of verbal abuse and soften the imprint they made on my heart and mind. God had preserved many relationships of family and friends that I had been cut off from, but I still did not know where I fit in to this life. Having been treated as less than human for so long, I was confused how people could see me and know who I was inside. In contrast, I didn't want people to see me and who I was inside. Hence, I felt invisible and thought I should be invisible. Therefore, I will continue this work until I am not afraid of my story. I have spoken about this in another poem, 'Goodness.' It is a feeling I wrestle with even now, in December 2022. Shortly before I wrote this poem, I started a new job. I had recently retired from 45 years of Pediatric nursing. My new job was in a place God had truly blessed to help suffering people see their life through the truth of scripture. During one of my training days, I had been meeting fellow coworkers and staff and became very emotional. I said to my friend who was training me, "I can't do this, there is too much goodness here", trying to hold back my tears. She asked if I wanted to leave but God supported me. "No, I really need to do this, I can do it". God provided this job when I was not expecting it and it has been a blessing to serve. I was not invisible to God. There is a particular Psalm that was shared with me on a few different occasions that helped inspire this poem.

He brought me out into a broad place;
he rescued me because he delighted in me.
Psalm 18:19, ESV

Feeling invisible
The memories telling lies
"You have no friends"
"No one cares about you"
"You can't do anything right"
God says no, I see you
He says do not listen to the lies
God calls me out
Takes my right hand
Come out into my beautiful broad place
You are safe
So, I walk and feel God's pleasure
Because he delights in me
Thinking… how can that be?
I am worthless
God says no, Jesus was pierced for me
For my sin
My iniquity
My sorrows
I walk…
I listen…
I see the beauty around me
And feel God's pleasure
He sees me
And I know…I am His

PURITY

As I started to bring my story to light and my sons and daughter shared some of their story, I saw that I needed to feel clean. On February 7, 2018, I wrote "I gave my whole self, loving and trusting to a man who could never love me." Through his manipulation and control, my identity was in him. Slowly in 2016 and 2017 God was showing me through his word that I could leave, be rescued and that my true identity is in Christ.

This poem was not written until August of 2020. On January 20, 2019, I made a journal entry about something I thought, "Not sure if I was dreaming, but I woke up thinking I needed scrub myself with sandpaper and bleed to be clean." I needed to shed blood to cleanse myself of the darkest abuse. Because these thoughts were a large part of counseling, many verses were shared to help me. When memories went in this direction, I would call on scripture, Psalm 129:2-4, Psalm 130:7, Psalm 131, and most recently, Hebrews 12:24, *"Jesus blood speaks a better word."* Counseling was making God's word louder than my dark memories. Jesus blood cleanses me and makes me pure.

In her blog, "Sexual Abuse in Marriage", Darby Strickland says, "Sexual abuse in marriage occurs when husbands make demands on their wives that are not based on love. 1 Corinthians 7:3-5 does not sanction these demands but is used as a goad to require a wife's compliance."[9] I believe that verbal and physical threats and abuse were used to foster my compliance so that I could not say no. Many women, like myself, do not realize this is what is happening until they are counseled. If you are a pastor or elder reading this, please know that this happens in Christian marriages. Leslie Vernick spoke at Westminster Seminary on domestic abuse to a class in Marriage and Family Counseling. A student in the M.Div. program questioned the validity of sexual abuse in marriage citing 1 Corinthians 7, because God said that a husband has the right to the wife's body whenever he wants. She went on to say, "Paul did not mean in these passages that a wife or husband can never say no."[10] No was never an option for me.

Heavenly Father, this is your new day
Out walking with you
Under the purity of your clear blue sky
This is the broad, safe place you brought me
I was angry
Words would not come
You said…wait
Hear my word
I hold your right hand
My heart is softening
I see a lone cloud in your pure, blue sky
There is some darkness in it
I see my sadness and pain there
You see it
You know it
You know each tear
Hold them in your bottle
I want to be clean
Need to be pure
You said…wait
Hear my word
My hope in you purifies me
Because you are pure
Holding my right hand
We walked….
On this beautiful day

WHO ALONE KNOWS?

As a pediatric nurse I knew what abuse was defined as but as a Christian woman I had spoken vows. I had promised God "till death do us part." We were married in the Reformed Episcopal Church. When you become a member in the RE Church, the church gives you "The Book of Common Prayer". On especially difficult days in my marriage, I would read the marriage vows at night by myself. I had made a commitment before God to honor and obey my husband but, he never "loved and cherished" me. My marriage was all work and responsibility to keep the man happy, to avoid his rage at all costs.

You may be thinking if I ever asked God why? Why did my life look like this? I do not believe I ever did at first. During my counseling process I would see close family members and friends with loving husbands. So many years spent loving the man and desiring the intimacy God promises in scripture, was not to be for me.

Gaslighting was not a word used in counseling, but it is helpful to explain my state of mind in the marriage. Things the man said and did left me confused, unable to make decisions, uncertain what was real or true, feeling like I was forever walking on egg shells. One powerful memory is of me standing in the kitchen, I have several tasks going on at once and I can't decide what I need to do next. My feeling of being alone many times was very powerful, but I see God never left my side.

"And we know that for those who love God all things work together for
good, for those who are called according to his purpose."
Romans 8:28, ESV

This verse was one of my favorite sermons that Dr. James Boice preached. It is true, whole sermons can be preached on one verse, Dr. Boice did it best. God worked out the hard things in my life together for my good. His timing was perfect.

Through God's ordinary, providential involvement, he is intimately and powerfully present in all of the details of our lives and world.
Todd Stryd, PsyD[11]

This quote gave me insight for my poem, and you will see its influence in future poems. Through God's *divine providence*, I persevered through 37 years filled with abuse and trauma. He allowed me to push through hard times to care for and love my children, work as a pediatric nurse in critical care and just flat out survive.

Am I not clay to be molded?
Do I not break?
But I also, am a treasure to be restored
I confess to Him
I cry to Him
He hears me
He knows my pain, my joys
He allowed my choices
Heard my cries
He is my sovereign God
Quiets my memories
In the darkest places he was there
It was for His purposes
His goodness
His steadfast love sustained me
In his sovereign grace he called me
Loved me
Rescued me
Redeemed me
And calls on me to say so….

GRIEF

For over two years I lived with my daughter, Kirsten, and her son. From November 2017 until January 2020. It was a blessing for both of us, as we both were struggling through many of life's difficulties. It was a joy to be able to help her and share in caring for my grandson. During this time Kirsten met a man named Carl and they were married in January of 2020. It was a beautiful celebration with family and friends.

It was another life changing event for me. This caused periods of sadness and grief that came in waves. During my marriage I had little time to grieve. I had no one to share in my grief or allow me time to grieve. For the most part, I stuffed this emotion down and would cry alone in my bed at night. The memories of past loss, sadness for the trauma my children experienced and thoughts of being alone for 37 years in a marriage came flooding back.

One of the hardest losses was my Dad's death in 1989. It was very sudden after a two-day hospitalization. At some point during the week prior his funeral, I was alone in the kitchen and the man came in and asked, "What is wrong with you?" I said, "I was just thinking of my dad." He responded, "let the dead bury the dead." This meant my time of grieving outwardly was over. I thought that it was okay because he had given me a few days, so whatever grief I had left, I buried with my Dad.

The three miscarriages I had was another difficult time when grieving was abbreviated. I was completely alone. At one point that man said, "You wouldn't have loved that baby anyway." Another time he said to my children, "I wanted this baby, but your mother didn't care." My second miscarriage caused him such anger, he dropped me off at the hospital alone for my procedure and afterward asked, "How do we know that it really was a miscarriage?" Insinuating that I had an abortion. All these things I kept inside and most I never shared until biblical counseling started. A miscarriage is a very personal and emotionally painful time for a woman. The first trimester of pregnancy is full of emotional, hormonal changes and doubts. Each new life is a gift and suddenly an unexpected loss. I needed the man for love and support, and he had none to give. I grieve over these precious lives even now.

Grief over the loss of my mother came at different intervals in life. I was the only child I knew through my school years whose mother had died. I didn't have a mother there for me by my side at different milestones in my life. None of the special times a mother and daughter spend together. I saw the grief in my father, but it was the 1960s and was not something that we talked about. My sadness and tears were held until I was alone in my bed at night.

As I processed things through counseling, I could see how God prepared me for the path before me. From a young age I understood that God was in the details of my life. He called me to be a mother to four sons and a daughter. All would come to call on Jesus as their Savior. God's light shined in our darkness, and he protected and rescued us. Early in 2020, grief came in almost unbearable waves, and I needed to put words to it before it overwhelmed me. A few other poems have reflected these thoughts, also. Words became God's gift to me to process and heal my hardest memories.

My chest is heavy
My throat is tight
Cannot stop the tears
God knows my heart aches
Jesus walks with me
Feels my pain
My Mom, God called her, so soon
Dad, loved and trusted, dearly missed
A man, abused my trust and loyalty
Stole God's promise of intimacy
His painful imprint, remains
Praying for the memories to fade
Three tiny babies
Loved, but never held
The man, father of my children
Dark
Evil
Unrepentant
God's light shines through
Jesus said, Come to me and rest
He holds me in the palm of his hands
Knows the depth of my grief
His strength for my weakness
His steadfast love, my comfort
I trust in Him
In times of grief
He sees me
Hears me
Is with me

NO FEAR

After I left for the last time, November 20, 2017, the man changed the locks on our house. I filed for divorce May 11, 2018, but would need a court order to enter the home without him there. My attorney advised against this because he could appeal the court order and I would need to see him before a judge which would cost more than I could afford to spend. Our attorneys agreed that I could enter the house accompanied by a non-family friend and that he could also be accompanied by a friend.

The defendant in a divorce case can delay the process through different methods, all legal. It took until October 2019 to arrange for me to get in the house. I had not seen or communicated with the man since November 19, 2017, so, I was fearful of this encounter. My counselor shared Psalm 56:3 and explained that it is not if I am afraid, but when I am afraid. I will be afraid, but I will trust in God. Fear is not a sin. Fear is an emotion. God was there for me. I wrote this poem on my walk the day after my counseling session at my favorite park. It is very peaceful there and many times I am alone.

When I am afraid, I put my trust in you.
Psalm 56:3, ESV

When I am afraid
I walk, I breathe
You lift my head
I look up to your heavenly places
Your sky, pristine blue with streaks of clouds
Like you painted them
I see your faithfulness to those clouds
Your steadfast love to the heavens
No fear!

When I am afraid
You hold my right hand
The shadow of your wings covers me
This new season
With your beautiful red, orange, and yellow colors
Comforts my soul
Your evergreens with branches reaching towards you
Show your strength
No fear!

When I am afraid
You know my name and…
I am yours
Tears start to come, you know my trouble
Your word comforts me
Your gentle breeze and warm sun bring a sweet smile
For your goodness
This walk in the beauty of your creation
Gives me strength in my weakness
No fear!

MY SECRET PLACE

Although much of what I have shared thus far has been about processing hard things which are reflected in my poems, I do have joyful times. Even in my marriage the man did not crush my spirit. I wrote in my journal on one occasion that it seemed like I was two different people, myself, and someone I did not know. A favorite verse during the early years of marriage was *Proverbs 15:13, A glad heart makes a cheerful face, but by sorrow of heart the spirit is crushed*". I was not crushed. God gave me hope in suffering and preserved me body and soul. Walking is so uplifting for me. It brings me joy, comfort and I feel safe. It is my secret place. This is just a special poem to share.

Today I opened my door and…
Went out into my secret place
Where God meets me and…
I see Jesus
Walking under the shade of large Oaks and Maples
Like under the shadow of His wings
I feel the breeze on my face
God collecting my tears
In my secret place, it is peaceful today
No memories of the past or…
Troubles of today
Just this moment
Listening to the song of the Cicadas
Rustling of the trees in the wind
Clouds of God's faithfulness
Floating across the sky
God promises to listen and hear
Just open your door and…
Call on Him

ON MY WALK

In scripture God uses His created world to speak truth to us, beautiful metaphors that bring us comfort and peace. After God rescued me in 2016, I started walking again. I was never much of a runner but walking and biking were always my favorite. Walking takes me to quiet places where I can ponder God's love and pray.

"But he would withdraw to desolate places to pray."
Luke 5:16, ESV

After my counselor shared Psalm 31:21, I searched for verses about God's steadfast love. Psalm 36:5, *"Your steadfast love, O Lord extends to the heavens, your faithfulness to the clouds"*, was a verse that gave me peace when my thoughts raced from memories. I would go on walks and ponder those verses. God reminds us of his "steadfast love" over one hundred times in scripture to give us strength in our weakness. I pray for that on my walks.

I go to my secret place
God meets me there
His word written on my heart

On my walk…I pray
Surrounded by his glory
He holds my right hand
I look to the heavens
God's steadfast love there
Fluffy, low clouds where…
I see his faithfulness

On my walk…by the creek
I watch the stream flow
Winding, peaceful in places
Then, working hard over the rocks
Tossing to and fro
Seeing it much like life
Life, winding through joys and sorrows

On my walk…I pray
Forgiveness for sin
Comfort for sorrows
Healing for suffering
Justice for evil

On my walk…
God's stream of living water
…Brings me peace

PONDERING

My counselor used the word ponder frequently. Because scripture speaks to everything in our life, I would often search for specific words, like ponder.

"But Mary treasured up all these things, pondering them in her heart"
Luke 2:19, ESV

Imagine Mary pondering giving birth to the very one who would redeem her people.
"Then all mankind fears; they tell what God has brought about and ponder what he has done."
Psalm 64:9, ESV

Thinking is one thing but pondering takes us deeper into our hearts and draws us closer to God. God preserved us body and soul and brought us to a broad, safe place.

Today I was thinking
It is a beautiful day for a walk
When I can ponder things in my heart
Pondering…is different than thinking
It goes deep in my heart
It asks why, how, and so much more
I see God's presence
On my path in life
If I ponder my path
God keeps my way straight
The why, is God's will
He directs the how by my steps
Because of his love for me
Standing on the bridge
I ponder the ripples in the stream
God directing their flow to the sea
I see the splendor of the world he gave us
His common grace
As I watch people coming and going
I see…
The perseverance and strength he gave me
On my path in life
Thoughts come and go
But… pondering with my heart
Is a gift God gives…me

REST

Let us with confidence draw near to the
throne of grace of grace, that we may receive
mercy and find grace to help in time of need.
Hebrews 4:16 ESV

Come to me, all who labor and are
heavy laden, and I will give you rest. Take
my yoke upon you, and learn from me for
I am gentle and lowly in heart, and you will
Find rest for your souls.
Matthew 11:28,29

Life in 2020 has been difficult. The world around us seems in chaos due to the Presidential election, violence in our streets erupting across the nation, Covid 19 lockdowns and social distancing. In our family life, Jeremy's and Kirsten's families moved to Kentucky and Virginia, respectively. I remain in our hometown with Jared to finish the divorce process.

Physical symptoms of my many years of stress persist. This year, ocular migraines returned resulting from years of fight or flight hormones constantly firing. Some panic like symptoms developed with tachycardia and difficulty sleeping. I needed rest.

My counselor had recommended the book *Gentle and Lowly* by Dane Ortlund but I did not want to spend the money for the book. I came across his podcast of "Gentle and Lowly" for free. He emphasized Jesus' "withness", not meaning "cool and detached pity" but rather "a depth of felt solidarity" in our distress.[12] The hard work of putting words to things in counseling can be exhausting. Coupled with the difficulty of my divorce process and emotional situations with my adult children and their families, I was tired. The words for this poem came quickly. When the memories will not stop, if you are in a place where you do not know what to do or how to do it, envision Jesus everlasting arms around you, and rest.

My life is a whirlwind
Trouble on every side
My mind needs rest
My heart is breaking
Jesus says…come to me
He knows I am sad and lowly
He will nestle me
In his everlasting arms
My tears seem…never ending
So…He bids me to come
His burden is light
In the quiet of my secret place
I call on Him
Jesus gives me rest
His compassion stills my heart
And…brings me peace

WE ARE HIS

As you can imagine having four sons and a daughter can create conflict in a family, especially as they become adults, marry, and begin life on their own. Each of my adult children are believers, know they need Jesus, but are at different stages in their sanctification. After I was rescued, and they each started processing their abuse, the inner family conflicts became exacerbated. I may repeat this in other poems because it is such a key issue in families of abuse, but the abuser goes to great lengths to pit family members against each other to retain control. It seemed that this problem persisted even though no one was communicating with him. My sons each tried to speak truth to him about his abuse, as did our pastor. He remained unrepentant and alone.

This was very concerning to me, especially since it was early 2020, and I had been out of the house for over two years. My counselor shared the words "complex pieces" to explain the conflicts between my family members. Through counseling I have learned to go to scripture for further explanation of things that I struggle with.

But we have this treasure in jars of clay, to show that the surpassing power belongs to God and not us. We are afflicted in every way, but not crushed; perplexed, but not driven to despair; persecuted, but not forsaken; struck down, but not destroyed. For this light momentary affliction is preparing for us an eternal weight of glory beyond all comparison.
2 Corinthians 4: 7-9,17, ESV

These verses have been an encouragement to me for many years, along with the words "complex pieces", my hope is that this poem will help my family better understand our conflicts.

We are in pieces
We are whole
It's complex
It's simple
Because…we are His
I am sorry for all
Couldn't see it
Clouded in the darkness
But…we were His
The pieces were cracked
Bruised
Broken
But not crushed
Because… we were His
Lord…why so hard?
So much work
The pieces don't fit
We can't be whole
We can…it's simple
Because…we are His
He gave us Jesus
Jesus fills the cracks
Comforts the bruises
Heals our brokenness
The pieces will fit
Jesus makes us whole
Restores our love
Because…we are His

UNITY

The Psalms or Songs of Ascents have been of particular help to me in my counseling. Sharing scripture in counseling has taken me on searches for the meaning of what I read more than ever before. I found that Psalms 129 through 133 were connected for me as I processed abuse and the abuse of my children.

"The plowers plowed upon my back; they made long
their furrows. The Lord is righteous; he has
cut the cords of the wicked. Let them
be like the grass on the housetops, which withers
before it grows up".
Psalm 129:3-6, ESV

This metaphor helped me put words to the shame of my abuse. There was a period of time I felt the deep wounds and imagined deep wounds in my back, dirty and bloody. My counselor emphasized that God cut my abuser off by my rescue. The Lord removed him like grass on the housetops.

Out of the depths I cry to you, O Lord!
I wait for the Lord, and in his word,
I hope; my soul waits for the Lord more
than the watchmen in the morning. With
the Lord the is steadfast love, with him there
is plentiful redemption.
Psalm 130:1-7, ESV

God hears my pleas for mercy and forgiveness. I wait alert and hopeful as keen as a watchman for the morning light because His steadfast love will bring plentiful redemption. God regards the gentle and lowly in heart and calms and quiets my soul to find my resting place in Him.

> *"This is my resting place forever; here*
> *I will dwell, for I have desired it."*
> *Psalm 132:14, ESV*

These verses came together to put words to our story from abuse to redemption and on to calming our souls and God providing rest. They flow right into Psalm 133 when our unity is restored. As stated in previous poem stories, an abuser sows division in their family to retain control. He pits the children against each other from a young age and remnants of division and strife persist in our family despite the man being cut off. Although not originally written for this purpose, these songs were eventually grouped together and sung on the road to Jerusalem for the yearly Jewish festivals. I like to use the same to explain our path from abuse and healing to love and unity.

We lived with a wicked man
His rage fostered
Strife
Division
Fear
Loving each other was hard
He wanted control
Dividing my children against each other
…and me
God didn't want this for us
But the man scarred our hearts and minds
Listen to God's word
The truth is there to find healing
His word encourages our unity
It will not be easy
The man afflicted you while very young
You are broken but, not crushed
I was there broken myself, but…
Trying to hold the pieces together
My heart aches for your suffering
Jesus desires our unity
Harmony essential to our healing
And our life
Beautiful to God like His valleys
Being nourished by the dew of Mount Hermon
God calling us to see His goodness
In our unity
Let the dew rest on us as God's grace
Beautiful, like lilies in the field
Giving us grace and love for each other
…and dwell together
In God's steadfast love

FLOURISHING

*"The righteous flourish like the palm tree and grow like a cedar
in Lebanon. They are planted in the house of the Lord; they flourish
in the courts of our God. They still bear fruit in old age; they are
ever full of sap and green"*
Psalm 92:12-14, ESV

As I processed abuse, I could see myself and the despair I lived in for many years. God preserved me. I see his steadfast love as I pushed through to care for my children, work as a pediatric nurse and the hard work of trying to diffuse and prevent angry situations. The verbal assaults were endless at times. "You are a coward", "You gave a false profession of faith", "You don't have any friends", "No one cares about you", "You disgust me", You never get anything right", "You're the worst liar I know", "Why can't you be like someone else", "You are a prude", "You had a sheltered childhood", "Why can't you be the Proverbs 31 woman." I have memories of myself, alone, crying silently, pushing through, and doing the work.

In the four years following God's rescue, I have done much painful work putting words to all these things, while at the same time having new things to process. God was moving quickly to bring our whole family story to light so the whole truth would be known. Things that came to light helped me make sense of many things that happened, or things that the man said that were very confusing. So many years later, my life made sense. He said things intentionally to keep me confused and in the dark about what was happening or who he really was.

It was necessary for me to process things that I had stuffed inside for many years starting with my childhood. Thinking was different in 1960 when my mother died. Everyone around me was grieving, I could see it, but no one knew how to talk to a child about grief. This is not said as a criticism but an observation from memories of my childhood. Often my counselor would mention my resilience and how I was flourishing. Despite my silent grief, I was in a loving family, and I was flourishing. The love I was raised in followed me into adulthood as a young woman, I flourished in my nursing career, loving and caring for men, women, and children. This was a gift. Then the man took it away.

It was a story of a life
A young, joyful life
Surrounded by her family
When sadness came
Jesus was there
Tears softened her wounds
Like the early rains
She was flourishing

The young girl grew
Knew God was by her side
Ordering her steps
Family and friends
Loving each other
In the quiet of the night
She asked Jesus into her heart
She was flourishing

The young woman
Joyful,
Loving
Caring
Working, helping
Men,
Women

Children
From her heart
These gifts God gave her
She was flourishing

The man changed her
His rage brought fear
Chaos
Confusion
His rage, unpredictable
She needed to diffuse
Protect
Surrender
It was her jail
She was in despair

God provided the way
For her rescue
Like lilies of the field
Rebirth and hope
Tears washing away the pain
Like the late rains
Producing fruit
Through God's word
I am flourishing…again

UNCHANGING AND RENEWAL

Life in 2020 started with the beautiful, joyful wedding of my daughter, Kirsten, being joined in marriage to Carl. The pastor who married my second son, Jonathan and his wife Alex said during the rehearsal, "a wedding is a forgiving ceremony." That thought stayed with me and I think of it now in relation to Kirsten and Carl's wedding. It was a celebration of love and uniting family members and friends for the first time in many years. My oldest son, Justin, escorted Kirsten down the aisle to her new husband. There was a bit of humor as, my son Jeremy's three-year old daughter and flower girl, would not walk down the aisle. Jeremy carried her and kindly helped drop her flower petals for the bride to enter. There was much joy and many tears that day. This was a very redeeming service.

Just two months later, 2020 was to change to a very hard season personally and for our entire country. A new Coronavirus would affect our country and the world population with grief and death globally, we haven't seen in decades. Social distancing, masks for all indoor encounters, universal lockdowns of businesses, schools, churches and canceling of all routine medical and surgical procedures left our lives changed for months to come.

In addition to the Covid 19 crisis, our country was in the midst of the 2020 presidential campaign. This would prove to be the most contentious election in history. There was distrust of the media like never before, all too much noise and difficult to process. There are two poems that spoke to me about this chaos, 'Renewal' and 'Unchanging".

UNCHANGING

The sky changed today
Pastel blue behind fluffy white clouds
Storms of yesterday, gone
The chilly breeze, refreshing
Walking, thinking how life changes
Storms of life tossing me about
God was there
His promises, sure
He never changes
Trusting, resting in Him
Under the shadow of his wings
In the cover of His tent
High upon a rock
He was there, unchanging
He held my hand yesterday
Holds it today
Holds my hand forever

RENEWAL

My thoughts are scattered
Feeling alone
So much information
I need to get outside
Walk in the sun's warmth
See God's glory around me
His season of renewal
Life springing up
Flowers blooming
Trees with new buds
Signs of creation's renewal
Comforts my soul
Like a baby in a mother's arms
Trusting and safe
Not alone
His Comforter…Spirit
Walking with me
He says don't listen to my fears
Listen to God's word
It's His season of renewal
Common grace revealed
…And be at peace

TIME

Often in my life I would think about time. What is time? How should we measure it? My now adult children, who experienced many things that should not have been, suffered anxieties and fears. This was a stumbling block at different times in their lives and they were afraid they wasted time. From a human standpoint, we may think time can be wasted but God uses time for his purposes. There was much help for me when Psalm 31 and 31:15 were emphasized one day in counseling. That verse inspired this poem on my walk the very day it was shared.

> *My times are in your hand; rescue me from the hand of my enemies and from my persecutors.*
> *Psalm 31:15, ESV*

What is time,

Minutes,

Hours

Days

Man would say yes

But time belongs to God

It is his gift of life

Not a measurement

He holds my time in His hands

I make plans but…

He directs my path

I see he was in each moment and…

There ahead of me preparing for

Hard things in my path

Time is a whole, not a part

It cannot be wasted

Because we trust a sovereign God

Each moment has a purpose

For His goodness

In joy

Laughter

Grief

Sadness

Fear

Pain

I see Jesus

Call on Him

He holds my times in his hands

NO PLACE TO GO

It is January 2021 and I have been counseling through my abuse for three years. A close friend at church, who had been in an abusive marriage for thirty years told me it takes up to half the time you are married to process all the abuse. I thought, I have a long road ahead.

Recently someone suggested, I enabled the man and was legally responsible, and cannot deny my role in the abuse. Things just got unbearably harder. I was powerless to enable the man. His power was his own. My actions and strategies were specifically used for diffusing his rage. Imagine a battle where you needed to be on alert for 37 years, God opens a door for your rescue and then you are told it was your fault. I felt like I could not keep my head above water.

Save me, O God! For the waters have
come up to my neck. …I have come into
deep waters and the flood sweeps over me.
I am weary with my crying out; my throat is
parched…waiting for my God.
Psalm 69:1-3, ESV

When he was reviled, he did not revile in
return; when he suffered, he did not threaten,
but continued entrusting himself to him
who judges justly.
1 Peter 2:23, ESV

The thought that I enabled, allowed, or permitted this abuse took me places mentally and emotionally I thought I had already processed, and I did not want to go back. Psalm 69 spoke to exactly how I felt. I saw through my research that there are women who counsel and tell women they enabled their abuser by the strategies they used to stay safe and diffuse the abuse. This is a very slippery slope and can place women in more danger. Christian women, in particular, who go to their pastor or elders with this approach, will be in more danger if they remain in the home with their abuser. The few times I called out my abuse whether physical or verbal, I escalated the situation.

In an earlier poem, I referred to the process of "traumatic bonding." This can be used to explain that an abused person does not enable their abuser. Lundy Bancroft explains that an abuser knows what he is doing, is intentional and his actions cause the abused person to become emotionally dependent on their perpetrator. In his book *Why Does He Do That*, he explains that no abuser is frightening or mean all the time and can be loving, gentle, humorous, even compassionate which makes the same person both rescuer and tormentor, "a bitter psychological irony."[13] No woman should be held responsible for this.

This is a difficult part of my story to share but necessary to dispute the enabling theory. At the time this happened, I did not know if this was possible, but I knew what if felt like. At the time, had I tried to bring this to light, there would have been no evidence. I would not be able to leave. I had no place to go. Life would become much more difficult.

> On a hot, summer night, the man was out late at a work golfing
> event. I was seven months pregnant with my fifth baby. Our down-
> stairs bedroom was very hot, so I decided to go upstairs on a
> fold out cot under the fan in my son's room. The three older boys
> shared a room, with two in a bunk bed next to where I was sleeping
> and one in a single bed across the room. They were seven, six and
> four years old respectively. Late that night the man woke me, did not speak a
> word, was violent and forced himself on me. I did not speak or make
> a sound and cried silently until he was finished. After he left the room,
> I knew what had happened, but thought, "is that even possible"?

Many years later, during a counseling session describing that night, I was finally able to call it "rape". I did not enable this, did not want this and to this day in 2022, it is a trauma I would like to forget. It is no longer an open wound, but has been debrided, and the scar is softening.

Trying to process the enabling thoughts, I wrote this poem in about fifteen minutes early one morning. These words came so quickly, I wrote this in the quiet of my room.

I had a wedding
But not a marriage
I said vows
Of love and commitment
No place to go

Scripture said to submit
Be loving and caring
Gentle and quiet in spirit
But he was harsh and cruel
No place to go

I tried
We fled for a time
There wasn't enough help
The pastor said, "it's safe"
No place to go

I used soft answers

The rage increased
Never fought back
His anger persisted
No place to go

My fear was real
My mind controlled
I couldn't think
No one to tell
No place to go

They are saying I "enabled him"
Allowed everything
Permitted the abuse
I am confused, in despair
There was…no place to go

How can that be
I can't understand
He cut me off
I was a shell of myself
No place to go

Besieged by the man
God was with us
His love, steadfast
Showed me the way
To find a place to go

AN ORDINARY WOMAN

Ordinary men and women are called by God to do the work for His kingdom. I am an ordinary woman, a sinner, daughter, sister, and mother. The wife of a man who would never love me as God intended. There were times after God rescued me that I would think about all the men in his life who knew of his outbursts of rage. Why God did not use one of these men to hold him accountable, was a question of mine.

I pondered these things for quite a while in counseling. My counselor had pointed out that I was never angry with God, but it is okay to ask the why question. As a young child, through a child's understanding, I saw God's plan for my life and am reminded of a quote I have mentioned in an earlier poem.

"Through God's ordinary, providential involvement, he is
intimately and powerfully present in all of the details of
our lives and world."[14]
Todd Stryd, PsyD

God reminded me of a scripture verse that helps explain the why question. In John MacArthur's book <u>Twelve Extraordinary Women</u>, he uses the same verse to explain one reason he wrote that book.

"But God chose what is foolish in the world to shame the wise;
God chose what is weak in the world to shame the strong;
God chose what is low and despised in the world, even things
That are not, to bring to nothing things that are, so that no
Human being might boast in the presence of God."
1 Corinthians 1: 27-29, ESV

In the man's mind, I was foolish, weak and by his actions he showed no love as God commanded him to. Husbands are called to love their wives as their own bodies. Abusers make you their property. God asked me to wait for his timing and to hold the man accountable.

After God rescued me, I thought
Where were the men
To hold the man accountable
There were many who knew
His violent abusive ways, but…
No one helped
Through pondering scripture
I could see that…
God called me, an ordinary woman
To do the work
God calls the "foolish"
To expose the "wise"
He calls the "weak"
To expose the "strong"
God gave me strength, soft answers
To diffuse the violence
He gave me perseverance
For the work and the waiting
Though the work was hard
The waiting seemed long
God called me, an ordinary woman
To be His instrument of redemption
To hold the man accountable
…To God be the glory

STAY THE COURSE

In a previous poem I said, "divorcing an abusive man is like amputating a diseased limb and you cannot get rid of the phantom pain". In May 2021, I am finding that metaphor to still be true for me. The man was served with the Divorce Complaint on May 11, 2018. In Pennsylvania there is a ninety-day grace period before any divorce can be finalized. After the ninety days if the defendant does nothing to agree or negotiate, the plaintiff needs to wait the remainder of the year before proceeding with filing documents to continue the process. So, May of 2019 my attorney and I decided on an equitable distribution of property and filed documents. The defendant needs to file the same documents, but he is given thirty to sixty days to file and has other ways to delay. As a result of this process, I continued to feel abused and controlled. In early 2020 my attorney filed documents for our first hearing with a court Master to discuss equitable distribution of our assets and debts. March 2020 the Covid pandemic hit, and the Pennsylvania Common Pleas courts were closed indefinitely.

Through counseling I came to see that divorcing the man would be exceedingly difficult. Mediation would not be a choice because it is not binding. The man remained unrepentant, telling my youngest son, Jared that he never touched any of us, "If your mother ever had marks on her, it happened at work". I was a Neonatal ICU and pediatric nurse who normally cared for children that were connected to ventilators and other devices. His unrepentance is deep within him. He believed that God provided our home for him alone and that God hates divorce. Through processing our abuse, we realized that selling the home through the division of assets would be beneficial to our healing, but this would take more time than we would like. Knowing that the man would revel in the idea that I would concede to his control, I needed to "stay the course." My time is in God's hands, and I will take courage and wait.

Scripture gives many examples of women who trusted God and persevered through trials. Sarah was a woman of perseverance and faith. Rahab, a woman rescued from a life of sin, became the first believer in Jericho and mother of Boaz, in the line of David and Jesus. I feel a particular connection to Rahab, as she protected the spies with her lies. I protected my children and myself with lies that I confessed in counseling. God did not count Rahab's lies against her. Many would say that God would have found another way to protect the spies if Rahab hadn't lied but if we believe God orders our steps, allows our choices, should we not believe that God used this for his purposes. Yes, I did lie to protect us from the man's anger, repented these lies, but believe it did protect us many times. I remain resolute in God's promise, *"hope in the Lord! For with the Lord there is steadfast love, with him there is plentiful redemption"*, *Psalm 130:7*

Sitting in the sun
At my favorite place
Where Jesus walks with me
I talk to him about hard things
We have met here many times
I am here now because…
I need to stay the course
There have been many years of hard work
God is closing that door
But I need to see this through
The man is resisting
Still telling lies
Lord, I pray for his heart to be weighed down
With guilt and shame
I pray for him to see
The pain he caused, and not rest
Father, give me strength
To stay the course
And finish the work
…to be free

ETERNITY

On a beautiful fall day
A young girl was sitting on a sitting on a swing
Thinking about eternity
Going there that day
So, no one would know
The dark secrets
She wanted the pain to stop
Death would free her
Here brothers were there
"What's wrong"
"Why are you sad"
"Talk to us"
No one sees
No one can know
She needed to keep everyone safe
The man might hurt them
Why does Mom not see, not help
"Mom you left me alone"
The young girl thought…
…I need to protect my family…
She had no answers for her brothers
She ran…he brothers yelling "stop"
She crashed the bike

Her brother yelling "no not my sister"
Her mother heard…she knew
There I am…kneeling in the street
Beside my daughter's lifeless body

This was from the memories of myself and my two younger sons who witnessed this 'accident'. It was a tragedy that all mothers fear at one time or another. My daughter suffered head and facial injuries that would heal but she lost memories prior to her 'accident' that would be restored years later after the birth of her first baby. God spared her life and kept her safe emotionally through her memory loss that she would do the work to process as an adult.

Due to her facial surgery and head trauma her first twenty-four hours were in ICU. I sat beside her, not sleeping at all, just watching her breath, and giving thanks to God for sparing her life. Her lower jaw was wired for a month and the day the surgeon removed the wires I held her hand and we cried together after each wire was pulled. We cried together all the way to the car. The truth and deceit has been revealed and the wounds are still raw at times but through God's grace the scars will heal and soften.

JOY IN CREATION

As an adult, especially after my wedding, God would remind me of verses I learned as a child. Many times, because scripture speaks to everything we encounter in life, I would just search a word or feeling for comfort. I have mentioned that most of my poems were written on my walks, so the beauty of the outdoors is spoken of frequently in them. I feel safe outside and I do most of my praying on my walks. There are just a few more poems to share that were inspired by scripture and the beauty of creation.

Wait for the Lord; be strong, and let your heart take courage; wait for the Lord!
Psalm 27:14, ESV

Your steadfast love, O Lord extends to the heavens, your faithfulness to the clouds.
Psalm 36:5, ESV

CLOUDS

Thinking of clouds
God's faithfulness there
There is so much to clouds
What they say to us
Yesterday, under a bright blue sky
They were light and fluffy, joyful
I saw long streaks of white clouds
Like God's arms reaching out with protection
Today, they are dark, low, and heavy
I see Jesus sadness for my heartache
Clouds full of moisture for a steady rain
Ready to cleanse, like my tears
Jesus is here with me
As I wait for the rain to come
To refresh my soul
The cleansing brings comfort
…for a time
As I look forward to the bright blue sky
I wait…
To see God's steadfast love to the heavens

THE STREAM

Standing on the bridge
Watching the stream
Water bubbling, working hard over the rocks
Ripples flowing out from the rocks
Hard and fast at first
Then slower
Easier
Gently
Spreading out across the stream
I see God's light shining
Over my hard work
Tightness and tears welling up
God is here
Tears flowing freely…more calm
Jesus walking with me
Taking the hard things
Softening the pain
Carrying it away
Like the ripples in the stream…

WINTER

Walking on a cold winter day
The sky, a mixture of emotions
Thick dark clouds filled with sadness
A brisk wind on my face
Parting the heavy-laden clouds
To expose a glad blue sky
The trees barren and exposed
Branches reaching towards the heavens
Crying out for renewal
The stream rushing faster
Searching for sun and warmth
Creation searching for hope in suffering
But… creation needs to wait
Winter brings a new year
A time for quiet and reflection
To ponder scripture
And see our hope is in Jesus
He is our hope in sin and in suffering
That gives us endurance for the days ahead
And we remain steadfast in hope
For just a little while
God will collect our tears
As creation waits for spring's renewal

WAITING

Lord you are my light
My salvation
You tell me "don't be afraid"
You keep me from wickedness
But…
You ask me to wait
To seek you with my whole heart
And…
Listen for your gentle whisper
From your word
Father you know my heart
I pray for your comfort
In my sadness
And…
In my waiting

TIME AT THE LAKE

Over the years after my wedding, I was cut off from family and friends who were very close to me. The man did this intentionally to gain control over me. I first contacted some of these friends and family through Facebook, so it was a blessing to see and speak to everyone. My stepmother and stepsisters were some of my first contacts. It was wonderful to hear from them and share what is going on in our lives. After God rescued me and I was free to see everyone, I was a bit fearful of the welcome I would receive since it had been so many years. God was gracious, it was like we had never been apart. The love and care I received was an encouraging gift from in-laws, my stepmother, stepsisters, cousins, and very special friends.

I wrote this poem during a vacation my daughter, grandson and I shared as a gift from my stepsister, Diohn at her home on a lake in Virginia. It was a respite from our trials at home, a peaceful time on the lake and a special memory.

The lake was peaceful, like liquid glass
With soft ripples from the breeze

The sky a beautiful blue
I knew God's faithfulness to the clouds

Time seemed to stand still
Knowing God's love, no tears need be shed

A daughter and a mother, together
Loving and laughing in the sun

Carefree and peaceful, away for a time
From the struggles of the heart

God was already there, ahead of us
With any need when we return to hard things of life

PRAYER

All through these last few years I had the desire to write a poem entitled "Prayer", but the words would not come. I have previously mentioned that scripture was used as a weapon and prayer as a punishment within my marriage. It took challenging work in counseling to be able to pray aloud. I have learned it doesn't need to be eloquent but only from my heart. Prayer is a quiet place in my heart and mind. God's answers come in quiet, small ways. You just need to wait and listen.

And after the earthquake a fire, but
the Lord was not in the fire. After the fire
the sound of a low whisper.
1 Kings 19:12, ESV

Prayer…
Is a place
And a time
In my heart
And my mind

Prayer…
When I cry out
God listens and hears
Jesus intercedes
Calms and quiets my fears

Prayer…
In my secret place
Wherever I am
God is beside me
His word dwells within

Prayer…
A time to repent
Mercy and grace
Freely given and…
Covers my sin

Prayer…
May not be words
Just a sigh
Or a groan
But…God hears and knows

Prayer…
If you ask
God will answer
His promises, sure
Take heart and…wait
For his gentle whisper

TEARS

You have kept count of my tossings;
put my tears in your bottle. Are
they not in your book?
Psalm 56:8, ESV

God gave us tears
Pure, cleansing waters
For our hearts, and…
Rainbows for our souls
Let them flow freely
Don't be afraid
God knows
Jesus is with us
Cleanse your sin
Your shame
Heal your grief
Your pain

Jesus is by your side
Let your tears flow
There are never too many
My tears seem endless
But…they are a gift
To purify my soul
Clear, living waters
Crying out to God
For strength and relief
This morning…
He dries my tears
Giving me strength for today
And…
A rainbow for my soul

CHOOSE LIFE

There were many days and nights that I struggled with the memories that I should take my own life. I shared thoughts early in marriage of taking the man's Valium and repenting immediately. Over the years my methods became more violent, and I repented many times for these thoughts.

I needed to put words to this again, to quiet my shame. When I put words to troubling things, I see God's providential care for me, my sons and daughter more clearly. I can envision the truth of scripture, God holding my hand and by my side, my refuge and protector. Through despair God was with me, with us, and I chose life.

Who was I
Before I was me
Still without form
But God knew me
There was a day
God gave me form
Made my life
To live for him
There was joy
Family

Relationships
Work
Play
I chose life
Joyful
Loving
Serving
Caring
Living for him
Then sadness came
Fear
Rage
Confusion
Isolation
I was in despair
Felt worthless
Life was work
For the man's pleasure
I thought of ways to end the pain
But… God said no
He gave me strength
Jesus with me
I chose life
The road was long
But I am free
I choose life…today

JUST BREATHE

God gave us breath, an essential part of living. When I am anxious and my mind is racing with memories of the past or the hard times ahead of me, I catch myself breathing faster. Through counseling I have learned that if I stop and concentrate on breathing, I am in the present and can draw on scripture to quiet my soul.

But I have calmed and quieted my soul, like a
weaned child with its mother; like a
weaned child is my soul within me.
Psalm 131:2, ESV

This verse is one I use on my walks when my mind is racing, and I need to just breathe.

Walking…
Breathing…
My heart pondering
Climbing my steep path in life
Like the hill in front of me
God comforts my soul and says…
Just breathe
Enjoy my common grace
The heavenly places
Bluest of blues
The tall Maples
Greenest of greens
And…
Just breathe
Standing on the bridge
I hear God's word

Remember…
"My steadfast love to the heavens"
I see some clouds moving in
His faithfulness is there
The ripples in the stream
Still carry away my sorrows
Just breathe
Draw near for mercy and grace
Comfort in my times of need and…
Just breathe
When my mind is racing
I stop… hear God's word and…
Just breathe

THE RIPPLES IN THE STREAM

Growing up in the Roxborough-Manayunk area of Northwest Philadelphia was an adventure. Fairmount Park, the largest urban park in the United States, was all around us. To add to the adventures of my childhood, Dad took us camping every summer to places like Cape Hatteras, Williamsburg, Jamestown, Florida, Ontario, and Quebec. Girl Scouts provided many outdoor activities; camping, bike riding, hiking, canoeing and those nighttime campfires with s'mores. I had a love for God's creation from an early age.

One day recently, in 2021, I was struggling with something challenging, my counselor reminded me of my thoughts about "the ripples in the stream." I have mentioned this in another poem, standing on the bridge watching the stream was a safe place where I met the Lord and prayed. The next day I thought this needs to be its own poem. The imagery has a calming effect for me.

On my birthday, several years ago, my oldest son, Justin, gave me a devotional, 'A Daybook of Prayer, Meditations, Scripture, and Prayers to Draw Near to the Heart of God'. I am currently on my third time through the book. This time around I gave particular attention to devotionals from Brother Lawrence, a lay monk of the 17th century. His teachings supported what I was learning through counseling that God is intimately present in all of our life and encourages us to call on God in prayer at any time.

*"You don't need to be in church all the time in order to
be with God. We can make a chapel in our heart where
we can withdraw from time to time and converse with
him in meekness, humility, and love".*
Brother Lawrence[15]

Where shall I go from your spirit?
Or where shall I flee from your presence?
Psalm 139:7, ESV

So, as you can see, I meet with the Lord in his place in creation when things got hard and I made a chapel in my heart. Take your sins and sorrows, open your door, find your stream, and let God carry them away, "like the ripples in the stream". His steadfast love is there for you, as it was for me.

I am free of the bondage
My jail is gone… I am free
When memories don't let go of me
God takes them away, flowing
Like the ripples in the stream

Memories pop up…
Why Lord?
It was so long… so hard
God promises to take them away
Like the ripples in the stream

Listen to God's word
He has cut the man off
He will wither like grass
Memories of him will fade
Like the ripples in the stream

I think of a river
The waters rushing fast
Dividing into streams
God taking painful memories
Flowing gently away…
Like the ripples in the stream

Heavenly Father please remind me
Your steadfast love was there
Is still here
Will always be here
For my memories to fade
Like the ripples in the stream

DARKNESS TO LIGHT

Where shall I go from your spirit? Or
where shall I flee from your presence?...If
I take the wings of the morning and dwell
in the uttermost parts of the sea, even there
your hand shall lead me and your right hand
shall hold me...even the darkness is not dark
to you; the night is bright as the day; for
darkness is as light to you.
Psalm 139:7-11, ESV

Life is a journey. In my journey God did not flee from our presence. Through the many years of abuse, God's hand held us, hiding us in plain sight. He was our light in the darkness. From the beginning of our counseling, we had talked about the need for our house to be sold. For many months we thought that would not be possible, until the Judge ruled in August 2021 that the house must be put on the market. An agreement of sale was signed in October 2021 with a settlement date of December. Praise God this path will be complete for our healing.

We needed to get in the house one last time while the man was working. My son, Jared and I went on November 4th with a police domestic standby. I had not been in the house for two years and was quite taken at how it made me feel. It had become the man's heart; a darkness was present. When we left I knew I would need a poem to speak about how I felt. My poems are the pieces of my life put together through scripture and biblical counseling. The pieces are becoming a whole, I see God's hand in getting myself back. Through several years of hard work God is closing this door to a new life for my sons, daughter, and myself.

I visited that dark place
Complete darkness now we are gone
The house is the man
Darkness to light…
His heart has taken over
So many years ago
I could not see the darkness
Jesus light was there
God with us
Our darkness as light to him
There seemed to be…
Love
Joy
Laughter
Amidst the…
Chaos
Confusion
Rage

God hid us in plain sight
Under his shadow
Days spent watching, waiting
Ready with soft answers
To calm the man's anger
And keep us safe
I couldn't always be there
Afraid of what could happen
Now…afraid of what did happen
My sons and daughter's story…
Cause my heart to ache
So many secrets
As God's word was opened to me
I saw the truth
It was the man's heart that spoke
Darkness there
It could not remain secret
Must be brought to light
So…God was there in our waiting
In time…he opened the door
And…
It was all brought to light
Redeemed through his steadfast love

MY BATTLE

There are days, even now four years after God rescued me, that I struggle with memories not letting go of me. It's something, as humans, we have no control over. At times, dreams take me back to my abuse. My counselor said, "This really is a battle." The man controlled my life and mind, but God did not allow him to take my spirit.

One day recently in May 2022, my son said, " Sometimes it's like you are not in the present." He had a timely observation and I responded, "Sometimes I feel like I am not in the present." I had the image of a revolving door, the present can't keep me out of the past or the past keeps me out of the present, both seemed true. This is my battle. It will be won with words God gives me to heal, dispelling the lies and quieting the memories. I knew this would need to be a poem.

The day my counselor shared the word "battle," I searched scripture and found Psalm 18, which has been a source of strength for me. I read verse 39. A few weeks later Revelation 3:8 was shared with me. These verses inspired this poem.

For you equipped me with strength for the
battle; you made those who rise against me
sink under me.
Psalm 18:39, ESV

I know your works. Behold, I have set before you
An open door, which no one is able to shut. I know
That you have but little power, and you have
Kept my word and not denied my name.
Revelation 3:8, ESV

It seemed like love
I tried to make it love
But…
I didn't see it
Couldn't see it
It was my battle
For my mind…my life
God gave me armor
Strength for my battle
There was no help
I felt alone
My battle raged
So many secrets kept
But…
God was always there
With strength for my battle
The years pressed on
I had little power
God by my side
Our very present help
Giving me grace to stand
In times of despair
His strength for my battle
Until he opened the door
For my rescue
Bringing my secrets to light
With words to heal my wounds
The work is hard
But…
With God's strength
I will win my battle to be…
Me!

MEMORIES

In this you rejoice, though now for a little while,
if necessary, you have been grieved by various
trials…obtaining the outcome of your faith, the
salvation of your souls.
1 Peter 1:6-9, ESV

The man has died. His name was John. On June 24, 2022, he was found in his apartment having died several days prior to being discovered. Providentially, I had talked in counseling about emotions I might have in the event of his death. Would any emotion be wrong or sinful. I was encouraged to know I could have any emotion, even relief, and no emotion would be wrong.

Prior to the man's death it had been difficult for me to desire or pray for God to grant him repentance. In the moments after being told of his death, God gave me the grace to hope that he may have known death was near and repented.

In the devotional, *Heart of the Matter*, Edward T. Welsh compares the tragedy, "Romeo and Juliet", to the comedy, "Much Ado About Nothing." He says, "You must decide whether you will live your life as a tragedy or comedy. The story Jesus offers you is a comedy. Scripture tells you the end, and if you have put your faith in Jesus rather than yourself, it is your end too. Jesus wins….For those who know Christ, life and joy are the last word."[16]

The hard memories will stay with me, but my work will continue to soften those that are past remembering those that bring a smile to my heart. Knowing Jesus was by my side these many years, I will have joy and live…

What are memories
Little slices of life
Many you want
Others you don't
But they make you
Who you are
God knew them
Before they were yours
The darkest threads
Weaving shame
You want them
To be gone but…
They won't leave you alone
Others bring joy
Loving memories
Smiles in your heart
Reasons to live
God uses them…all
To make you His own
You only need to
…Call on Him and
…Live

WHOLE…AGAIN

Towards the end of 2022 my desire to be whole again was powerful. In other words, to reclaim myself. After five years of work, I was still putting the pieces together, feeling like I was still stuck between the past and present. I have used the words "thread of abuse" before in my story. The image of a sticky spider web and all the thoughts of who the man was and what he did have me stuck there.

Over a year ago during a low point for me, wanting to give up, Mark 3:27 was shared with me. Seeing the work God was giving me to hold the man accountable, to be able to say "no, enough," and be required to sell the family home that he told us God gave him, gave me renewed strength for my work. On January 1, 2023, during my morning devotions I wrote this poem as a result of a prayer I had written while reflecting on the previous year.

But no one can enter a strong man's
house and plunder his goods, unless he
first binds the strong man. Then indeed
he may plunder his house.
Mark 3:27 ESV

On this first day
Of this new year, 2023
I sit by myself
In the early morning hours
Wanting to be whole…again
God meets me here
He knows this has been a long road
So much work has been done
To bind the strong man
To soften the man's imprint
The power belongs to God
His will is done
The man is gone from this earth
No more threat or torment
No fear of crossing his path
Seeing his angry face
In God's goodness and…
Steadfast love…
I am free but…
There is more work
More words to speak
To keep the boxes closed
To be whole…again
To God be the glory!

EPILOGUE

For I, the Lord your God hold your
right hand; it is I who say to you,
"Fear not, I am the one who helps you."
Isaiah 41:13 ESV

I have set the Lord always before me;
because he is at my right hand, I shall
not be shaken.
Psalm 16:8 ESV

If I take the wings of the morning
and dwell in the uttermost parts
of the sea, even there your hand shall
lead me, and your right hand shall
hold me.
Psalm 139:10 ESV

My story, told with poems and prose, started with me in the grip of the man. As my story unfolded through my writing, I now see that we were always in God's grip, holding our hand and lifting us up. Isaiah 41:13 is the first verse that was shared with me by my counselor. I never read this verse before and so I needed to know more. Why the right hand? Further study explained that the right hand or right side is synonymous with goodness. In Isaiah 41:13 God leads our way, helps us when are weak or fallen, encourages us and so he holds our right hand. As a nurse I took this one step further, in our created bodies, our blood returns to the heart from the right side of the body. I envisioned God's goodness flowing through our heart in times of trouble preserving us body and soul. In our oppression and abuse, God never let us go.

One day after counseling on a walk, I was thinking of my work in the Neonatal ICU, and I saw a parallel between counseling an abused woman and caring for a premature baby. Both have suffered pain that should not have been. The baby should be safe inside the mother's womb. The woman safe in the arms of a loving husband. The baby's body is fragile and easily wounded. The woman's heart and mind are fragile and easily wounded. Each must be handled gently, carefully so as not to cause more damage, allowing healing. Time is a friend of both with liquid nourishment for the infant and spiritual nourishment from scripture for the woman. Imagining these parallels helped me see that I would need time and hard work to heal. I drew courage from the precious lives I cared for, each fighting to live the life God gave them.

Over the years in counseling and processing my story I have come to see how important it is for the Church to understand how to help abused women and their children, especially considering our broken family court system. Lundy Bancroft quotes statistics in his book *Why Does He do That*, only 5% of abusive men can be rehabilitated and that figure is generous.[17] If the man "professes faith", he will be two different people deceiving Church leadership. Abusers have a contemptuous personality that is reserved for their intimate partners. It is not that they are unable to change; they are unwilling to change and give up their power and control. Abusers are very adept at seeming remorseful and repentant, while remaining the same person. I can speak to personal experience here until I realized it was only an act, as did my children. Through my story you have seen that, thankfully, God put people in my life when my story was brought to light to seek justice for me.

If your first question was, "Why doesn't she just leave?," my hope is that you see how difficult that is for a woman. When children are involved the problem is compounded because of the real possibility the courts will award partial custody to the father placing them in greater danger. As Darby Strickland in her article, "Four Reasons Why Women Stay in Abusive Relationships," all the usual reasons were true for me; "Not understanding the severity of our danger, lack of family, church, and community support, leaving is the most dangerous time, leaving abuse is extremely difficult and costly."[18] After I left in 1991 he was threatening upon our return, our abuse increased and at the time there was "no place to go" indefinitely for me and my five children. As a Christian woman, I had taken vows before God and believed I was to stay. The man knew this and abused my trust and loyalty.

Before closing my story, I would like you to see through my poems how biblical counseling was instrumental in processing my abuse and that work continues today in 2023. I have come to define biblical counseling as "The sword that makes the wounded whole" from the hymn "O Church Arise."[19] I believed from a young child that God was in the details of my life and God would need to be in the details of my healing. God's providential care brought me to a place where my biblical counselor opened scripture and walked with me through this hard work.

One more goal I hope to meet is for the commitment of the Church to come alongside abused women and children. Having been left on my own in 1991, my church did not understand oppression and abuse or how the man deceived them. You need to "Stay the course." Dr. Carl Trueman said in lectures at Westminster, California March 5, 2019, "The first time a woman tells her pastor of her abuse it is only about twenty percent of her story."[20] Things that she says will seem impossible but know that they are true. Open your doors and hearts and please believe her.

If this is story is yours don't let your fear or shame keep you from bringing your story to light. Open your heart, cry out to God, He will hold your right hand and lead you to a place and person to walk with you in your healing to become whole…again.

In conclusion, I see God's plan for my life, the love he gave me in motherhood, loving my four sons and daughter, the gift of caring for people in their tiniest beginnings and now loving my thirteen grandchildren. God has always been there by my side, protecting me and my sons and daughter and giving me endurance for my path in this life. He rescued us each in his providential timing and stays with us on our road to healing with Jesus filling the cracks and brokenness. To God be the glory.

Strength and dignity are her clothing and
she laughs at the time to come.
Proverbs 31:25 ESV

BIBLIOGRAPHY/ENDNOTES

Preface

1. Dr. Carl Trueman, Sermon March 20, 2016, Cornerstone OPC, Ambler PA
2. Lundy Bancroft, Why Does He Do That, Penguin Putnam Inc. 2002, 7
3. Dr. Liam Goligher, sermon Beauty and the Beast, July 10, 2016, Tenth Presbyterian Church, Philadelphia, PA
4. Ten Boom, Corrie. *The Hiding Place.* (Chosen Books, November 1971)

New Life

5. Bancroft, Why Does He Do That, 3

Who Am I

6. Bancroft, Why does He Do That, 220-221

Sons and Daughter

7. Bancroft, Why Does He Do That, 220
8. Jennifer Michelle Greenberg, OPC Open Letter Regarding Abuse, Part II: The Last Writhe of the Devil, jennifergreenberg.net/2020/04/20

Purity

9. Darby Strickland, Sexual Abuse in Marriage, Part I, CCEF Blog, June 6, 2018
10. Leslie Vernick, How Do I Know if I'm Being Sexually Abused in My Marriage, leslievernick.com, Jan. 24, 2018

Who Alone Knows

11. Todd Stryd PsyD, God's Providence and Human Agency in Counseling, The Journal of Biblical Counseling, Vol. 33/Number 3, 48

Rest

12. Dr. Dane C. Ortlund, Gentle and Lowly 14-day Podcast, Day 4, Draw Near

No Place to Go

13. Bancroft, Why Does He Do That, 220-221

Ordinary Woman

14. Stryd, God's Providence and Human Agency in Counseling, 48

Ripples in the Stream

15. Brother Lawrence/Alan Vermilye, The Practice of the Presence of God, Brown Chair Books 2021, Letter 7,32

Memories

16. Edward T. Welsh PhD, Heart of the Matter, Daily Reflections for changing Hearts and Lives, New Growth Press 2012

Epilogue

17. Bancroft, *Why Does He Do That?, 354*
18. Strickland, Darby. Four Reasons Why Women Stay in Abusive Relationships, ERLC.com, June 9, 2021
19. Chris Tomlin/Keith Getty/Stuart Townsend/Kristyn Getty, O Church Arise, Worship Together Music, Thank You Music Ltd., S.D.G. Publishing, Sixsteps Songs
20. Dr. Carl Trueman, Miles to Go Before I Sleep, Reflections on Church, Seminary and Bi-vocational Ministry, March 5-6, 2019, Westminster Seminary, CA

Printed in the United States
by Baker & Taylor Publisher Services